INTERACTIVE PRAYER JOURNAL.   ELEVEN SESSIONS

Praying beyond the borders

PRAYERS that INVITE YOU TO SPEND TIME with GOD ON BEHALF OF OTHERS

WANDA RITCHEY

authorHOUSE

AuthorHouse™
1663 Liberty Drive
Bloomington, IN 47403
www.authorhouse.com
Phone: 833-262-8899

© 2021 Wanda Ritchey. All rights reserved.

No part of this book may be reproduced, stored in a retrieval system, or transmitted by any means without the written permission of the author.

Published by AuthorHouse 07/14/2021

ISBN: 978-1-5246-0767-8 (sc)
ISBN: 978-1-5246-1503-1 (hc)
ISBN: 978-1-5246-0766-1 (e)

Library of Congress Control Number: 2016909988

Print information available on the last page.

Any people depicted in stock imagery provided by Thinkstock are models, and such images are being used for illustrative purposes only.
Certain stock imagery © Thinkstock.

This book is printed on acid-free paper.

Because of the dynamic nature of the Internet, any web addresses or links contained in this book may have changed since publication and may no longer be valid. The views expressed in this work are solely those of the author and do not necessarily reflect the views of the publisher, and the publisher hereby disclaims any responsibility for them.

Wanda Ritchey

Dedication

First, I would like to honor God for every blessing and every gift that he has bestowed upon me. I am humbled to be able to share my experience with prayer as a way of life for me. I count it a great privilege to share how the power of prayer has sustained me and has brought me into a more loving relationship with an all-powerful God. To my two adult children, Juan and Ayana, I love you immensely. Thank you for bearing with me during my extended seasons of prayer and consecration. I am grateful for the times that you guys prayed with me. You are my gift from God that I will always cherish.

Pastor Shaun Saunders, thank you for believing in me. It was your encouragement daily and speaking the word of God into my life that propelled me from a place of passivity to a place of productivity in completing this project and more. I joined your 90 Day Challenge and spent those days from 5:45 a. m. till 7:00 a. m. in praise, worship and reading God's word. After each session you gave a commentary along with "Worship Work" for daily implementation. That whole process kept me going when I wanted to give up and felt the task was insurmountable. Your dedication to God's calling in your life inspired me to continue the writing process, keep praying, preaching and to pressing into my new place in God.

To my parents, Ozzie Mae Ritchey-Palmer, and David Ritchey (deceased), thanks for teaching me how to have faith, to walk with God and how to stand in the face of adversity. To my siblings, Juanita, Angela, David Jr., Dwight, Nicholas, Elliott, Alicia, Alphonso, and Marianne … it's the experience.

"Sisterfriends" are treasures. Thanks for my power-pushers, my accountability partners, Yolanda Ratliffe, Jacqueline Lawrence, Zaquisha Green, Sandy and Monica Daniels, Zabrina Gordan, and Gwendolyn Richards. Even with great distance between us, you have been there for me continually.

Special thanks to Greenlawn Baptist Church of Columbia, South Carolina. You adopted me as your Sunday School teacher at a time when I had hung my teaching ministry on the shelf. Iris, Evelyn, Mary, Carolyn, Shirley, Joye, Lia, Jackie, Norma, Margaret, Francis, Elaine, Annie, Lois, Carol, Cora, Tillie, Scarlette, and Linda, you guys are the best. I love you all dearly.

Preface

I grew up in Miami, Florida with my parents and eight siblings. As a young girl, I use to watch my mother as she would steal away to her bedroom to pray. She would sometimes kneel down in front of the light blue papasan chair and have long conversations with God. She would tell him how she desired to be like him and ask him to make her better. I even witnessed her sometimes crying and asking God to help other people, to heal and to provide for them. This was intriguing to me because I've always had a tender heart for others as well. I wanted to know how I could tell God about my pain and the pain of others so that life could be better. Most importantly, I had a desire to know the power of prayer.

When I became an adult and left my parent's home, there were many times when I needed answers from God or direction for a major decision I had to make. I realized the same God who would answer my mother's prayers was listening to my voice as well. He kept shielding me from situations that would have otherwise been detrimental to me. I was assured time after time that he was not far from me and that he loved me. When I didn't know how to deal with lack, fears, parenting or just day to day choices I could go to God in prayer and find solace. It was during my times of struggles, pain, heartaches, and disappointments I discovered that God saw me as his precious child and was attentive to my cries. I began to see how my circumstances were being used to catapult me into a place beyond just me. It showed me that a loving God was teaching me with life experiences what it meant to walk close to him, commune with him and to be sensitive to his leading.

During my eight years while serving in the U.S. Armed Forces, I had to rely on God's strength to carry me through tough times and even times of uncertainty. It was through my prayer life that I was sustained, comforted, encouraged and used to be a pillar for fellow soldiers. There is no other way that I could have survived or thrived during that season in my life without constant communing with God.

When I first learned that my next set of orders was for Riyadh, Saudi Arabia, I knew that it was certainly praying time. It was one thing to pray from the comfort of my home where I had most things at my fingertip, so to speak. But it's another story when you're being taken to a foreign land with the pending call for war. I was a newlywed, and I had my newborn son to care for. It was certainly a time when I needed to pray for more than my immediate needs.

Through many life experiences I've learned that prayer for me is a calling. I became an ordained minister in 1999 and joining the intercessory prayer team was unquestionable. By then I knew it was the place for me to be. I felt at home because I had spent years leaning and depending on God to walk me through this thing called life. I had experienced how he would bring change for others through prayer. I'd even coupled prayer with fasting so that the focus was shifted from what my flesh desired to what God wanted to do or say. This growth proved very rewarding and gratifying. I then began to look at the lives of others who valued prayer and I started reading materials that would help me to grow in my understanding of the role of prayer in my life not only as a believer, but also as an intercessor. As time passed, I saw the need to pray beyond my immediate needs or just for things that only impacted my welfare. I witnessed God working on behalf of others who I was intentionally including in my prayer times. This encouraged me to learn more about intercession and to serve as a part of the church prayer ministry so I could learn to work with teams of persons with the same passion to see others helped, delivered and set free from the grips of the enemy.

I remember watching a movie entitled *War Room*. One of the main attractions for me was the fact that the "war room" was a place specifically designated for the character to go when she wanted to spend time talking to God. I found it very interesting that she placed emphasis on going there daily and she shared how it was one of her favorite rooms in her home. Although I didn't call it a "war room", I used my bedroom walk - in closet as a place that I could always go during my prayer time. However, I knew that the day would come for me to have a formal prayer closet. When I bought my retirement home, I turned one of the spare bedrooms into a "War Room". I even bought a sign from one of the local Bible bookstores and placed it on the door. It's almost like they do not disturb sign on the library conference room.

Now I go into my War Room and stay as long as I want and spend time praying "Beyond the Borders" of just my personal concerns. I have the privilege of intervening on behalf of all people groups, all nations, all mankind. The needs, the lists and the concerns are ever growing. As a result, I have shared in this interactive journal some of my personal prayers and have invited you the reader, to join me on this beautiful journey of communing with an almighty and ever-loving God.

Thanksgiving

Lord, thank you for your unfailing love toward us daily. We sense it through your presence, kind acts of forgiveness and through your unmerited favor. Praise you for being the creator, the giver of life, and the almighty God. There is none beside you. No one can copy nor replace you. You alone are the only wise God and redeemer of us all. Everything we will ever need is in you.

We're grateful because our life is hid in you Lord Jesus. We cannot be plucked out of your hand. There is no test, trial nor circumstance that can separate us from your love. We bless your name because you thought enough of us to save us and rescue us from the enemy. Then you cleansed us from unrighteousness because you chose us to serve you and to bless others.

Thank you for always making yourself available to us. There is never a time you do not hear the cries of your children. Help us to always be conscious of your presence and to understand that no power can overtake us because of who you are. Let us be reminded that through our praise we have the victory over all things. Cause us to always be mindful of your blessings which are many. It is you who gave us life and for that we are grateful.

Jesus, we recognize and accept you as the Savior of the world. You are God's only Son who sacrificed your life so that we might live by submitting to your word. We can't thank you enough for the various ways that you:

- Provide for us
- Keep us
- Watch over us
- Feed us
- Direct us
- Chastise us
- Revive us
- Enable us
- Equip us
- Sanctify us
- Rejoice over us
- Intercede for us

Continue steadfastly in prayer, being watchful in it with thanksgiving. – Colossians 4:2

Giving thanks always and for everything to God the Father in the name of our Lord Jesus Christ. – Ephesians 5:20

"And I give unto them eternal life; and they shall never perish, neither shall any man pluck them out of my hand." – John 10:2

Things to Consider

1. What are some specific things God has done for you that you are grateful for?

2. Discuss a time that you needed God and he revealed himself to you.

3. How many ways can you think of to say "thank you" to the one who makes all provisions for you? List at least five.

4. Where can you insert a "praise break", a time to just say thank you Lord, during your day?

    Try to vary your methods and places throughout your week.
5. Why is it beneficial to have a grateful attitude?

Personal Prayer of Thanksgiving

Reflections/Testimonials

Intercession

Abba Father, you are a holy and loving God. It is a privilege and honor to serve you. We rejoice in your desire to save all mankind. We stand in the gap for your people everywhere. Lord we pray on behalf of those who are broken and don't know how to regain the momentum to move forward. You are the only one Lord who can revive and give new life. We are depending on you to mend and to make whole again.

Renew a passion in your people to see souls saved, delivered, and set free from the clutches of the enemy. Prepare the hearts of men everywhere to receive you as their Lord and Savior. Through your lovingkindness, allow every experience, circumstance and adverse situation to draw men unto you. Let the oil of your anointing destroy yolks and burdens and cause men to seek you for their way out.

We know that apart from you, oh Lord, mankind is lost. Let your word find a place in the hearts of men that will arrest everything that tries to separate them from that which you have predestined for their lives. Look upon nations that are experiencing war and those who are sacrificing innocent lives for selfish gain. Give shelter for your people and a way of escape for those who trust in you. Be a refuge in their times of distress. Let those who are free remember to travail for those who are in bondage.

Lord, send a revival that will shake the nations like never before. We need a revival that will again cause men to ask, "What must I do to be saved?" We need your mercy God for those who are suffering from hunger, disease, natural disasters and constant turmoil. Lord let the people begin to see you in every aspect of life. Let the cries of the people be for your mighty hand of deliverance. Forgive us for blaming you and help us to depend on you!

It is you alone God who can make the difference in this dying world. There is neither hope nor help aside from you. Bring about a change that will bring glory to your name and cause men to acknowledge you for who you are. You are still King of kings, Lord of lords, Prince of peace, and the great redeemer!!!

We continue to intercede on behalf of:

World /Church leaders	Lost souls	Families
World hunger/disasters	Government	Missionaries
Sex trafficking	U.S. Armed Forces	Education Systems

*And I sou*ght for a man among them that should make up the hedge, and stand in the gap before me for the land, that I should not destroy it: but I found none. -Ezekiel 22: 30

Praying always with all prayer and supplication in the Spirit, and watching thereunto with all perseverance and supplication for all saints. – Ephesians 6:18

Things to Consider

1. Is there anyone in your sphere of influence who has a need for your prayers?

    - List their names and needs
    - Commit to pray for them for 1 week
    - Note any answers to your prayers

2. How would their lives be impacted if remembered them consistently during your daily prayer time?

3. What changes would you like to see in your family, community, or workplace?

4. Where would you like to see some positive changes in the world around you?

5. Why is intercession necessary?

Personal Prayers of Intercession

Reflections/Testimonials

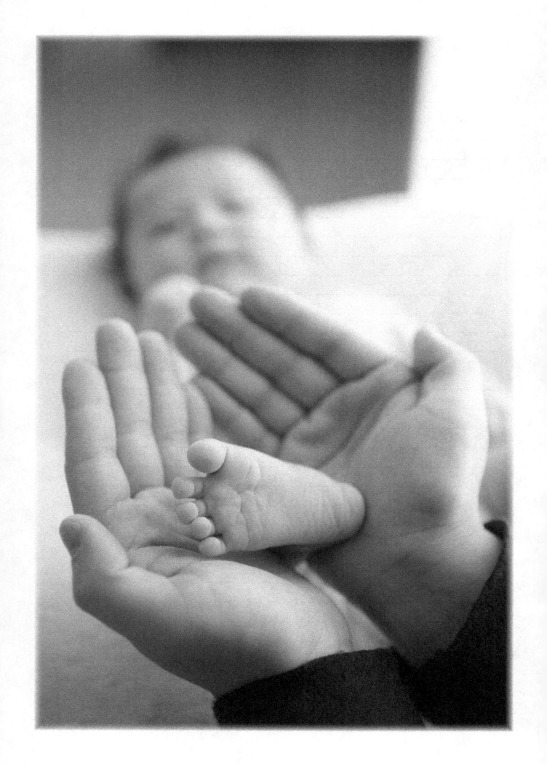

Protection

God our creator and redeemer, thank you that we can run to you for shelter at all times. With grateful hearts we adore you because we are never without hope. Kind Father let us be reminded that our safety is in you alone. In a time when the world is in a chaotic state, you are aware of all that occurs. There are various ills in our societies causing many to fear. Let us meditate on your word day and night for in it we'll find rest for our souls (Matt. 11:28) and a hope that all things are in your control.

Make us cognizant of the many battles that you've already won. Fear cannot be an option for those who trust in your sovereignty. Lord, continue to cover us when our hearts feel faint, circumstances seem gloomy, and it appears that the enemy is winning. Help us to know what it truly means to stand still (Psalm 46:10) and to depend on your deliverance.

Father we need you to keep our families from contention, poverty, substance abuse, and immorality. Protect our homes from robbers, murderers, rapists, and disasters. Protect our minds and bodies from the subtle attacks of the enemy who wants to destroy all that you have planned for your people to experience and enjoy in this life. Cover our country and give wisdom to those who make decisions regarding the safety of America. Turn our hearts to you again so that we can operate under your blessings.

Thank you that there is safety in your arms. Help us to run there for our protection. In the night seasons of life, let your light shine through reassuring us of your presence, your power and your promises. Your presence alone silences our enemies. Your power crushes the head of our enemies, and your promises assure us that the enemy is already defeated!!! Thank you that we can make our habitation in you, a place where your power supersedes the powers of anything or anyone pitted against your chosen ones. So Lord, be our constant protection we pray.

The Lord is my light and my salvation; whom shall I fear? The Lord is the strength of my life, of whom shall I be afraid? —Psalm 27:1

The Lord shall preserve thee from all evil: he shall preserve thy soul. —Psalm 121:7

Things to Consider

1. What are some key scriptures that demonstrate God's protection for his people?

2. When have you experienced God's protection in your life?

3. What is the role of prayer and God's protection?

4. Where is the ultimate place of safety and how is it acquired?

Personal Prayer for Protection

Reflections/Testimonials

Guidance

Lord we thank you for your omniscient power which we can rely on for direction. Thank you that it is your desire that we don't go astray. You said that your sheep know your voice so teach us to be quick to give heed when you speak and to obey. Help us to be diligent in praying concerning all of our affairs and to always invite you to have the leading role. Make plain to us the ways in which you speak for every situation. Let us be conscious of the many distracters and to readily dismiss them so that we can be aligned with your desires for all matters.

Give us clarity on what pleases and displeases you so that our lives will always bring you the glory. Lead us to your holy hill where we can always find you. Forgive us for the times that we relied on friends and beggarly elements rather than relying on you. Show us how to cast our concerns upon you to avoid going through the same situations repeatedly. Though the devil presses in on us daily, let us look to you and not try to take matters into our own hands.

Today's leadership is in need of your divine intervention globally. Let the spirit of the living God be present in every board room, in every meeting session that impacts the lives of your people. Turn the hearts of every leader to you Lord. Let your power be manifested till it drives out the spirit of manipulation, craftiness, and selfishness from leaders. Give them a heart for the people and cause them to be more sensitive and concerned about the welfare of all. Let your lordship be evident among the nations where there is strife and division. Bless leaders everywhere to be open to hear a word from you that will transform their mindset to reflect your will in the earth. The burden for leadership is evident in the rising numbers of leaders who are abandoning their posts and some even committing suicide because of the pressures.

Dear God, let your power reign and give strength and reassure that the battle belongs to you. It was never your desire for the weight to be on the shoulders of the leaders. According to your word, the government is on your shoulders (Isa. 9:6). Let leaders everywhere be reminded of this. You are the only one who can bring about such transformation so hear the cries of your people and do the supernatural within today's leadership for your glory.

Give us clarity concerning the things that both please and displease you so that our lives will be aligned with your desires for us. Lead us to your holy hill where we can always find you. As we come to various crossroads in life, let us meditate on your word that assures us of your continual guidance (Isaiah 58:11). Cast the devil out of our minds so that all of our steps will be directed by your Holy Spirit. Let the truth of your word have preeminence over every voice we hear. Help us to make decisions that will bless us and glorify you, oh Lord.

I will instruct thee and teach thee in the way which thou shalt go. I will guide thee with mine eye. - Psalm 32:8

Teach me to do your will. For you are my God. Let your good spirit lead me on level ground. Psalm 143:10

Things to Consider

1. What are some ways that God gave instructions or guidance to his people in the Old Testament?

2. Does God still give direction to his people today?

3. Why is it necessary to pray before making major decisions?

4. Who are some of the people within your inner circle that you can rely on for godly counsel?

5. Do you feel that it is necessary to consult God for daily direction?

Personal Prayer for Guidance

Reflections/Testimonials

Divine Destiny

Heavenly Father you are holy and righteous with the ability to chart the course of mankind, your creation. There is no shadow of changing with you because you're immutable. You are from everlasting to everlasting. For those things we are grateful, and we know that we can trust you with our past, present and future endeavors.

You have chosen us and no matter what tests or trials we encounter, your plan will supersede them all(Ephesians 1:14). By your power you will do all that is necessary for us to reach the place that you have predestined for us. Cause us to turn our eyes on you so that distractions will not become hindrances to your plans for our lives. It is your desire that we reach our full potential so give us a level of trust in you that will propel us into a God - place. Take us to that place where doubt is arrested and our past can no longer hold us hostage. You are Lord of all so nothing is great enough to keep us captive or prevent us from walking in the fullness that you have promised us.

Let us think as you think, see as you see, walk as you walk and hear as you hear. We desire for your plans for our lives to become a daily reality. Cast out fears that try to cripple us or make us focus only on our meager strength. Our hope is in you because you are the almighty one who can make the difference in our every situation. You promised to supply all of our need so help us to depend on your provision. You said that you would never leave us nor forsake us so help us to be mindful of those things as we move toward our hopes and dreams to succeed.

We rebuke everything that the enemy poses as a threat to our success in you and in this life. We speak peace to every storm that is designed to take us off course. We speak to every mountain to move and that every obstacle would be subject to God's anointing which destroys every yoke. Lord let your power be revealed in us. Your power is more than enough to strengthen our faith, cause us go above and beyond our plans, be more than conquerors, stand in the face of adversity, and to walk into our destiny.

Before the mountains were brought forth, or ever thou hadst formed the earth and the world, even from everlasting to everlasting, thou art God. —Psalm 90: 2

For thou art my hope, O Lord God: thou art my trust from my youth. — Psalm 71:5

Things to Consider

1. What does God say in scripture concerning your future?

2. When is the last time you consulted God concerning his purpose for your life?

3. Do you feel that you are using your gifts and talents to full capacity?

4. What has hindered you in the past from reaching your God potential?

5. How will things be different as you begin to walk in your pre-destined place?

Personal Prayer for Divine Destiny

Reflections/Testimonials

Youth

Gracious and Holy Father, we honor and adore you. We give you thanks and praise for the youth of today. It is evident that you care for them and want them to walk in total surrender to your word. Let your glory fall upon them and cause their every desire to be for the things of God. There are many things that come to confuse their paths but you oh Lord will make the crooked straight in their lives. Let God arise and the head of the enemy be crushed so that your children can realize and walk in your will for their lives. Let them be surrounded by God-fearing persons who are not afraid to speak into every dark corner of their minds to drive out evil and all ill intensions from the enemy.

Dear Jesus, break every fetter, every chain that impedes their process. Strengthen their inner man so they can stand in the face of adversity. Teach them how to persevere and stand until you manifest their deliverance in every area of their lives. Let the peace of God overshadow the storms they encounter. Let them experience the joy of the Lord in place of sorrow. Let depression be far from our youths.

Lord let them encounter your love that heals, delivers, and makes them brand new. We depend on you to sever the ties of all relationships that don't propel them into the place you've predestined for them. Give protection over their minds, bodies, and even their desires in order for them to reach their destiny and avoid defaulting to what the enemy puts before them. Allow your glory to be upon them daily.

As the youth experience your presence we know that a transformation will take place that only you can give, oh Lord. Because you are full of compassion, change the course of their lives and reposition their aspirations for a bright future in you. Make straight the things that are out of kilter because you know their ending from the beginning. Surround them with your favor that will open great doors of opportunity that they otherwise would not experience. Shut the doors that are not a part of your plans for them.

The blood of Jesus covers the youth!!! The word of God is being taught to them and as a result they have great peace. We decree that the light of Christ shines upon them guiding their steps daily. We declare the youths are becoming more and more conscious of the ways of the Lord and they choose to follow the ways of righteousness. Every unclean spirit that fights against them is rebuked and the word of God brings life everlasting to our youths. Thank you Lord that your word is already settled in heaven concerning them. Therefore, we trust you to make the difference in their lives.

I will go before thee, and make the crooked places straight: I will break in pieces the gates of brass, and cut in sunder the bars of iron. -Isaiah 45:2

For we have not an high priest which cannot be touched with the feeling of our infirmities; but was in all points tempted like as we are, yet without sin. -Hebrews 4:15

Things to Consider

1. What are some of the things that the youth have to contend with today?

2. Who do the young people tend to turn to for help?

3. How are the youth of today impacted by the media?

4. Why do you think many young people are walking around aimlessly?

5. What is the role of the church and our youth?

6. How can your input help to bring change for the younger generations?

Personal Prayer for Youths

Reflections/Testimonials

Elderly

We give thanks to our God who is omniscient, omnipotent, and omnipresent. Every day comes with great expectation of your new mercies for your people. You keep proving to be a compassionate, caring and faithful God. We thank you because you watch over your people. We are grateful for the men and women who have set examples of righteous and wholesome living more multiple generations. Bless now those who are elderly and in need of care.

Dear Lord there are many who don't have insurance or the finances to meet their basic medical necessities. Look upon them and prove yourself as Jehovah Jireh, the Lord who sees and provides. We need you to be a rock, a shelter, a refuge, and a helper for your precious ones who are ripe in age. Replace their fears with a great trust in you. Where they have doubts let them once again have great faith in you. Where they may have grown cold, let them again have a great love for you. Forget not your children as you alone can keep their minds sharp, their bodies strong and their surroundings stable. Nothing is beyond your power or to difficult for you!!!

Continue to place people on their paths that will be sensitive to their needs. Give them people to many along their journey. Although some seniors have been abandoned by family and they suffer from the lack of love and the feeling of belonging, you promised not to leave nor forsake them. That is more than enough! So help them to trust in your word to keep and care for them perform for them continually? Thy will be done according to your great pleasure.

Be a fence, a fortress around the elderly and restore them to a place where life still has purpose, great meaning. God you are still strong to deliver! Let them experience your joy no matter their state of being. Prove yourself again and show your hand strong giving them the grace to trust in you alone. Deal with the things that contend with them. Perfect the things that concerns them even as you have promised. Let old age be a blessing as they receive the honor they deserve.

Rekindle in us a heart, a burden, and a renewed concern for the elderly. Yes, one that will cause us to return to them and care for their daily needs. Make us a blessing to the weak and feeble. Turn our hearts again to remember those who have taught us the ways of the Lord. Your word tells us that it is more blessed to give than to receive. So let us give of our substance, out time, and our genuine consideration to those up in age. In doing so, we know that it will be pleasing in the sight of God.

And Abraham called the name of that place Jehovah-jireh: as it is said to this day, In the mount of the Lord it shall be seen. -Genesis 22:14

The Lord is my rock and my fortress, and my deliverer; my God, my strength, in whom I will trust; my buckler, and the horn of my salvation, and my high tower. -Psalm 18:2

Be strong and of good courage, fear not, nor be afraid of them: for the Lord thy God, he it is that doth go with thee; he will not fail thee, nor forsake thee. -Deuteronomy 31:6

I have showed you all things, how that so laboring ye ought to support the weak, and to remember the words of the Lord Jesus, how he said, It is more blessed to give than to receive. Acts 20:35

Things to Consider

1. What are some areas in which the elderly need support?

2. Whose responsibility is it to care for the elderly?

3. Do you have elderly persons in your family who need to experience God's love?

4. How can you extend yourself to demonstrate God's concern for the elderly?

Personal Prayer for the Elderly

Reflections/Testimonials

Success

Kind and caring Father, you are holy and full of splendor. The whole earth is covered with your glory. You are our creator and redeemer so we give you the praise. We bless you with our mouths, our hands and our hearts. Thank you for creating all that you did for mankind to enjoy and to have dominion over. We know that our times are in your hands. We realize that without you nothing was made, developed. Our lives have no purpose outside of you heavenly Father. Life would be null and void without you at the helm – no direction. Your guidance is essential for the direction of all mankind.

It is because of you, O Lord, that men can strive for better or to achieve greater accomplishments. Your word tells us that apart from you we can't achieve anything (John 15:5). Our hope is in you because you alone can cause us to increase. So let us always keep you in remembrance as you bless us. Let not pride nor self righteousness, nor haughtiness consume us as you bless us.

Drive the enemy away and keep us from the evil one who does not want to see us prosper. Shield our families and let your angels war for us as we move forward in the things that you have for us. Bless us to keep our focus on you so that we will not be distracted from our greater. You intended for your people to prosper so let it be. You intended for us to be successful so let it be. You intended for us to enjoy the fruit of our labor so let it be. Let nothing block the good life that you desire and designed for your children.

We know that we are mere stewards of the positions we receive in life. Help us to continue to walk in humility and give you praise for all things. It is you who open doors that would otherwise be shut in our face. It is you who make the provisions when things are not even within our human reach. It is you who even gives us the power to get wealth (Deut. 8:18).

Your word declares that you will withhold no good thing from those who walk upright (Psalm 84:11). Thus let our character be one of integrity, righteousness, and faithfulness. Help us to be grateful to you and forgiving of others. It was you who caused Daniel to be promoted for his consistency in serving you. It was you who saw fit to crown David as king rather than his siblings. You are the same God whose heart is still for your people. Now cause us to be successful and let every promotion be orchestrated by you according to your time, due season.

I am the vine, ye are the branches: He that abideth in me, and I in him, the same bringeth forth much fruit: for without me ye can do nothing. —John 15:5

But thou shalt remember the Lord thy God for it is he that giveth thee power to get wealth, that he may establish his covenant which he sware unto thy fathers, as it is this day. —Deut. 8:18

For the Lord God is a sun and shield: the Lord will give grace and glory: no good thing will he withhold from them that walk uprightly. —Psalm 84:11

Things to Consider

1. What are you most passionate about?

2. Do you depend on God or your own intellect for the success of your endeavors? Elaborate.

3. How can you show appreciation to God for your dreams, visions, and ideas for success?

4. Should others be blessed by your success or is it just for your personal gain? Explain.

Personal Prayer for Success

Reflections/Testimonials

Provision

God of the universe and creator of all living things, we bless your holy name. You have made man in your likeness for which we are grateful. Forgive us for every time that we have sought for our needs to be met by any other. You have proven yourself to be a God of abundance. Our joy, peace, salvation, strength, shelter and substance all comes from you.

There is nothing that your children need that you cannot provide. You are the same God who provided for the children of Israel during their wilderness experience. Do the same for your children today. You are the same God who delivered Daniel from the lion's den and provided him with a greater status to receive all that he needed and more. Do it for your children today. You brought Joseph out of the pit and set him in the palace where he ruled. Lord of lords, do it for your children today! God you chose Esther's life to save the lives of her people (Esther 4:14). Use your people today to cry out once again for the salvation of others.

You make all things available to those who recognize who you are and trust you for all things. Thank you for knowing what we have need of (Matt. 6:7, 8). Many are losing their loved ones. Give us comfort in times of sorrow and provide direction. This is a time when the world is in utter chaos and people are disillusioned. You are a God of order and nothing takes you by surprise. Manifest your sovereignty everywhere, to all people.

Revive the church to a place of trusting none beside you. Let your power be demonstrated again through your people. Let the word of God be preached till the needs of the people are manifested. Drown out the voice of the enemy through your word, O Lord. Drive out demons that come to keep the people in bondage. Shower your blessings of plenty, blessings of deliverance, blessings of spiritual gifting, blessings of healing and joy in the Holy Ghost.

When the way seems bleak, let us keep our focus on you as our provider, our way of escape, our loving Father who keeps his promises. Help us to always be mindful of your presence where all things are made accessible to your people. Make us conduits for the rest of the world to receive your blessings because you dwell in us. Cause nations to take notice of how you continue to provide for your people, thus giving them a desire to know and serve you Lord.

And Abraham said, My son, God will provide himself a lamb for a burnt offering; so they went both of them together. – Genesis 22:8

Trust in the Lord with all thine heart; and lean not to thine own understanding. -Proverbs 3:5

Things to Consider

1. What are some specific things that God has provided for you?

2. How do you seek the Lord to see if what you are asking him for is in alignment with his desire for you?

3. When do you pray for God's provision?

   - When the need first arises?
   - At the point of crisis?
   - When all else fails/
   - Constantly?

4. Why is dependence upon God so vital for our every provision?

Personal Prayer for Provision

Reflections/Testimonials

Warfare

Abba Father, gracious, merciful and mighty are you. Bright and morning star we worship your holy name. You're king of kings and the lord of hosts, ruler of everything. Because you are sovereign we can trust you to win every battle, and all that opposes your kingdom. You're God of heaven and earth and everything is subject to your word.

Teach your children how to quickly discern enemy activity and how to stand guard in the spirit. Let your word have preeminence over every test and trial that we are confronted with. Keep us from all manner of evil. Cover our minds so that the enemy will not be able to win even in our thought life. Give us the mind of Christ in all things.

Cast out fears and doubts and make us ever conscious of your holy presence. Demons cannot withstand your presence. All powers are subject to you and are at your command. Nothing and no one can stay your almighty hand. You cause your warring angels to fight for your people. Help us to be reminded of all that we have at our disposal because of your shed blood.

We decree that we are more than conquerors in Christ Jesus (Rom. 8:37). We are covered with the armor of God which enables us to stand against the tactics of the enemy (Eph.6:11-17). There is no power that can overtake us because you are greater than them all, oh Lord. You are our shield and we have a hiding place in you (Psalm 119:114).

As your children, we denounce any thoughts of cowering down from our enemies. We stand strong in the face of adversity knowing that you are with us, oh God. We rebuke sickness and disease and declare that by your stripes we are already healed Isaiah 53:5). Send your anointing to destroy every yoke of bondage, every evil thing that tries to attach itself to the people of God, and every unclean spirit (Isa.10:27).

By the power of the Holy Ghost we come against depression, poverty, lack, and fear of the unknown. Satan, loose your hold on the minds of God's people! For we declare that we have the mind of Christ therefore you are still a liar (1 Cor. 2:16). We walk in God's promises and there is no good thing that we don't have access to. All of our needs are met and we operate in abundance for every area of need in our lives.

We refuse to worry about the future because the word of God stands forever!!! God's word is all we need to defeat every demon, every evil work, including every spirit of doubt. The blood of Jesus cleanses us through and through. Thus we walk in the liberty which has already been won through his shed blood. For his blood covers us, his word shields us, his Spirit comforts us, and his promises reassure us!!!

And it shall come to pass in that day, that his burden shall be taken away from off thy shoulder and his yoke from off thy neck, and the yoke shall be destroyed because of the anointing. — Isaiah 10:27

Thine, O Lord, is the greatness, and the power, and the glory, and the victory, and the majesty: for all that is in the heaven and in the earth is thine; thine is the kingdom, O Lord, and thou art exalted as head above all. -1 Chronicles 29:11

Things to Consider

1. Do you have a team of people who cover you in prayer? Generate a short list.

2. Do you believe that spiritual warfare should be a concern for today's church? Why or why not?

3. How is spiritual warfare addressed in the scriptures?

4. When did Jesus encounter battles with the enemy?

5. How did Jesus respond to the attacks of the enemy?

Personal Prayer for Warfare

Reflections/Testimonials

Family

We give praise to you Lord for your creation of the family structure. Thank you for your design for mankind to procreate for your glory. Down through the years there has been evidence that you bless those who honor you. Let it be the desire for families to put you first again. Help us to go back to the basics of praying together, loving and considering one another. Take us back to the times when it was important to read your word together in our homes and expect your blessings upon our families.

Don't let us walk in ignorance concerning the enemy's desire to destroy the family structure. Let our eyes be open to his tactics so that we will be able to persevere and take our rightful places. Cause fathers to know what it means to be the head of the household. Bless wives to desire their husband and children to love and respect their parents (Eph. 6:1-2).

Let the light of your word shine upon our hearts that we will reflect you in al of our doings toward one another. Give the children a listening ear for that which is right. Bless fathers to lead according to your guidance. Bring back unity, love, peace and prosperity to those who dare to trust you, O Lord.

We curse and denounce spirits of selfishness, discord, hatred, disrespect and greed within our families. Let every filthy thought and deed be far from us.

Strengthen the hearts of single mothers and single fathers to take a stand for your righteousness and not waver. Bless those who are married with a longing to put you first so the blessings will flow from breast to breast. Let the oil of your anointing be evident in every home, every community, every region where families honor the Lord.

We curse the spirit of drug abuse, verbal abuse, physical abuse, emotional abuse or abuse in any form. We expose every demon that will try to abort the family structure in any way. The word of God is against you!!! The blood of Jesus prevails over you now and you have no place in our minds, our homes, our affairs, our dreams, our desires, or our plans. Our steps are preordained because we trust our Lord. The God of peace goes before us and our destiny is beyond the control of the enemy. We speak the favor of God over every family and decree that God is for us.

And all Judah stood before the Lord, with their little ones, their wives, and their children. -2 Chronicles 20:13

But the mercy of the Lord is from everlasting to everlasting upon them that fear him, and his righteousness unto children's children. - Psalm 103:17

What shall we then say to these things? If God be for us, who can be against us? -Romans 8:31

Things to Consider

1. How can we ensure unity in our families?

2. What are some things you would like to see manifested for your family?

3. Why does the enemy attack families?

4. Describe some ways that you can add strength to your family?

5. Commit to accepting family members who need more time to grow.

6. Find various ways to communicate God's love toward your family.

    - Send a card of encouragement
    - Try an uplifting phone call
    - Give a compliment
    - Design a personal gift
    - Show gratitude
    - Say a prayer for them each time you think of them

Personal Prayer for Your Family

Reflections/Testimonials

CPSIA information can be obtained
at www.ICGtesting.com
Printed in the USA
LVHW020703020821
694217LV00001B/115